P9-DGV-167

GOOD

dgs

MJF BOOKS
NEW YORK

Published by MJF Books
Fine Communications
Two Lincoln Square
60 West 66th Street
New York, NY 10023

Good Dogs
Library of Congress Catalog Card Number 99-74460
ISBN 1-56731-348-5

This edition published by arrangement with Andrews McMeel Publishing.
Edited by Sheila Buff
Designed by Pat Tan
Produced by Smallwood and Stewart, Inc., New York City

Credits and copyright notices appear on page 70.
Printed in Singapore on acid-free paper

MJF Books and the MJF colophon are trademarks of Fine Creative Media, Inc.

10   9   8   7   6   5   4   3   2   1

INTRODUCTION

"All knowledge, the totality of all questions and all answers, is contained in the dog."

— FRANZ KAFKA

I often take my two dogs for long walks through the woods and fields near our house, returning along a quiet country road. Our walks are leisurely, with many investigative pauses along the way. At every stop, the dogs find a richness of information in scent and sound that I can only dimly perceive, even with my higher intelligence and superior vision. Together, we find more and learn more — and have more fun — than we do alone.

Humans and dogs have been walking together though the woods and fields for thousands of years. From the dawn of civilization, we have been partners in a relationship that goes far beyond mere mutual survival — it is a special bond. We love our dogs, and they love us.

That special love, a love unique to humans and canines, has been celebrated in words and art that cross cultures and centuries. Dogs have always been important figures in art and literature, much admired for their fidelity and loyalty. The ancient Egyptians depicted the god Anubis with the head of a dog. In the Odyssey, the faithful old dog Argus is the first to recognize long-lost Odysseus on his return, and in Celtic lore, Cavall was King Arthur's favorite hound.

In more modern times, many well-known authors have praised their dogs in prose and poetry. The poet Matthew Arnold wrote memorial poems to his dachshunds Geist and Kaiser. Elizabeth Barrett Browning wrote a wonderful poem of gratitude to Flush, her cocker spaniel companion of fourteen years. Lord Byron eulogized his Newfoundland dog Boatswain in a moving poem and had the dog buried in the tomb he intended for himself.

The sentimental dog stories of Albert Payson Terhune, Jack London, Zane Grey, Ernest Thompson Seton, and many others are still popular and widely anthologized. The delightful true-life tales of James Thurber, E.B. White, James Herriot, and Daniel Pinkwater, among many others, sparkle with memorable dog personalities.

The love dogs inspire comes through even in the non-fiction works of those who study and train them. This is evident in the works of Konrad Lorenz, Barbara Woodhouse, Elizabeth Marshall Thomas, and Gary Paulsen. The sheer joy of being so close to dogs resonates in every word.

Editors rarely get to work on something they truly love—and I love dogs, real and imaginary. Gathering the quotations for this book was a real pleasure, a reason to revisit favorite authors and an inspiration to discover new ones. The words that were chosen are those that reveal all that is finest in the nature of our closest animal companion.

SHEILA BUFF

ogs are...wonderful. Truly. To know them and be with them is an experience that transcends—a way to understand the joyfulness of living and devotion.

Winterdance
GARY PAULSEN

He seemed neither old nor

young. His strength lay in his

eyes. They looked as old as the

hills, and as young and as wild. I

never tired looking into them.

An Adventure with a Dog
JOHN MUIR

. His strength lay in his eyes.

and as young and as wild. I

H   nor

ves   s the

d.   nto

young. His strength lay in his

lls, and as young and as wild.

FOUR DOGS NOT ONLY SEEM,

BUT ARE, A GREAT MANY,

and I wasn't surprised by my relations' comments. What, though, they didn't know was the excessive pleasure, amusement and exercise I got out of them. True the exercise sometimes appeared to be a little much, and when I was tired I was inclined to think that perhaps I ought to have started on this sort of thing younger; but anyhow the eighteen months during which all four were with me were much the gayest and liveliest, if also the most breathless, of my life.

I would recommend those persons who are inclined to stagnate, whose blood is beginning to thicken sluggishly in their veins, to try keeping four dogs, two of which are puppies.

All the Dogs of My Life
ELIZABETH VON ARNIM

We are alone, absolutely

alone on this chance planet;

and amid all the forms of life that

surround us, not one, excepting the dog,

has made an alliance with us.

Our Friend, the Dog
MAURICE MAETERLINCK

DOG PEOPLE HAVE THE COMFORT *of at least some part of their lives that can be done over and over, again and again, without the anxiety of getting it right, rewriting, revising. A contented life for a dog is a repetition that holds no boredom or disappointment. Walk, Biscuit, Drink, Nap,*

and so many other happy recurrences—
they're all positions on the face of a dog's nat-
ural clock. And even though each dog finally
disappoints us with its death, we are the ones
who call it untimely, wishing and willing the
repetitions to outlast our longer lives.

Dog People
MICHAEL J. ROSEN

The great pleasure of a dog is that you may make a fool of yourself with him and not only will he not scold you, he will make a fool of himself too.

Dogs
SAMUEL BUTLER

What a wonderful indicator of happiness is the dog's tail; the half-mast wag with the very tip of the tail, showing nervous expectation; the half-mast slow wag of the interested dog who wants to know what master is saying but doesn't quite pick it up; the full-mast wag of excitement and happiness when he is really happy; and last but not least, the tail between the legs of the nervous, shy or unhappy dog who trusts no one and to whom life is a burden.

No Bad Dogs
BARBARA WOODHOUSE

buy a pup and your
money will buy
Love unflinching that
cannot lie.

The Power of the Dog
RUDYARD KIPLING

Here one day would stand a giant among dogs, powerful as a timber wolf, lithe as a cat, as dangerous to foes as an angry tiger; a dog without fear or treachery; a dog of uncanny brain and great lovingly loyal heart and, withal, a dancing sense of fun. A dog with a soul.

Lad: A Dog
ALBERT PAYSON TERHUNE

dogs

love company.

They place it first in their
short list of needs.

My Dog Tulip
J.R. ACKERLEY

'Tis sweet to hear the honest watch-dog's bark

Bay deep-mouthed welcome, as we draw near home;

'Tis sweet to know there is an eye will mark

Our coming, and look brighter when we come.

Don Juan
LORD BYRON

I could never quite take dogs for granted. Why were they so devoted to the human race? Why should they delight in our company and welcome us home in transports of joy? Why should their greatest pleasure lie in being with us in our homes and wherever we were? They were just animals after all and it seemed to me that their main preoccupation ought to be in seeking food and protection; instead they dispensed a flow of affection and loyalty which appeared to be limitless.

Dog Stories
JAMES HERRIOT

The dog is the

god of frolic.

HENRY WARD BEECHER

HOW TO LIVE WITH

1. DO make sure your dog understands
   what you mean. Use proper grammar
   and enunciate your words clearly.
   Dogs disdain sloppy language.

2. DON'T try to communicate with
   your dog in his own language for
   purposes of saving time. Barking
   does not come easily to people.

3. DO discuss problems with your dog.
   Dogs prefer persuasion to force.
   If you see him yawn, stop.

A NEUROTIC DOG

4. DON'T forget: you cannot live
   with a dog who is not housebroken.
   You must move out.

5. DO show your dog what it is
   you want him to do: jump, roll over,
   fetch a ball. Dogs learn more
   by first-hand observation than
   from textbooks.

 STEPHEN BAKER

i

myself have known some

very profoundly thoughtful dogs.

The Thurber Carnival
JAMES THURBER

One reason a dog is such comfort
when you're downcast is
that he doesn't ask to know why.

ANONYMOUS

To call him a dog hardly seems to do him justice, though inasmuch as he had four legs, a tail, and barked, I admit he was, to all outward appearances. But to those of us who know him well, he was a perfect gentleman.

HERMIONE GINGOLD

The dog has got more fun out of Man than Man has got out of the dog, for the clearly demonstrable reason that Man is the more laughable of the two animals. The dog has long been bemused by the singular activities and the curious practices of men, cocking his head inquiringly to one side, intently watching and listening to the strangest goings-on in the world. He has seen men sing together and fight one another in the same evening. He has watched them go to bed when it is time to get up, and get up when it is time to go to bed. He has observed

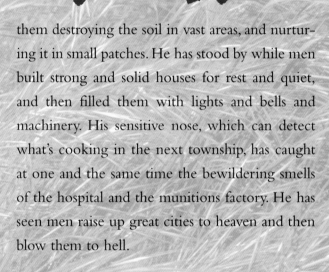

them destroying the soil in vast areas, and nurturing it in small patches. He has stood by while men built strong and solid houses for rest and quiet, and then filled them with lights and bells and machinery. His sensitive nose, which can detect what's cooking in the next township, has caught at one and the same time the bewildering smells of the hospital and the munitions factory. He has seen men raise up great cities to heaven and then blow them to hell.

The Fireside Book of Dog Stories
JAMES THURBER

THE FIDELITY OF A DOG

demanding no less binding moral
responsibilities than the friendship
of a human being. The bond with
a true dog is as lasting as the ties of
this earth can ever be.

Man Meets Dog
KONRAD Z. LORENZ

IS A PRECIOUS GIFT

The small percentage of dogs that bite people is monumental proof that the dog is the most benign, forgiving creature on earth.

The Koehler Method of Dog Training
W.R. KOEHLER

If you pick up a starving dog and make him prosperous, he will not bite you. This is the principal difference between a dog and man.

Pudd'nhead Wilson
MARK TWAIN

I came across a photograph of him not long ago, his black face with the long snout sniffing at something in the air, his tail straight and pointing, his eyes flashing in some momentary excitement. Looking at a faded photograph taken more than forty years before, even as a grown man, I would admit I still missed him.

My Dog Skip
WILLIE MORRIS

O

f all the dogs whom I have
served I've never known
one who understood so
much of what I say or held
it in such deep contempt.

One Man's Meat
E.B. WHITE

A dog lives in the moment

And always hopes for the best.

Little Dancing Dogs
JACK BROWN

Humans have externalized

their wisdom—stored it in museums,

libraries, the expertise of

the learned. Dog wisdom is inside

the blood and bones.

Nop's Trials
DONALD McCAIG

Among God's creatures two, the

sizes and all the shapes, in order not

dog and the guitar, have taken all the

to be separated from the man.

ANDRES SEGOVIA

*I*t was a perfect spring day, gold and blue and green. We felt good. After a while, I began to realize that the dog and I were sharing a thought. It wasn't anything very special or complicated—it was something a man could think, and a dog could think. It was something like. . . "Ahh!"

Fish Whistle
DANIEL PINKWATER

Histories are more full of

examples of fidelity of dogs

than of friends.

ALEXANDER POPE

There is no age-limit
in this matter of loving a
dog or being loved
by a dog. No one is too
young or too old to
love a dog or to be loved
by a dog.

Bunch
JAMES DOUGLAS

a c k n o w l e d g m e n t s

Excerpt from *Investigations of a Dog* by Franz Kafka. Reprinted by permission of Random House, Inc.

Excerpt from *Winterdance: The Fine Madness of Running the Iditarod*, copyright © 1994 by Gary Paulsen, reprinted by permission of Harcourt Brace & Company.

Excerpt from *All the Dogs of My Life* by Elizabeth von Arnim. Reprinted by permission of Little, Brown and Company.

Excerpt from *Dog People: Writers and Artists on Canine Companionship* edited by Michael J. Rosen. Copyright © Michael J. Rosen. Reprinted by permission of Artisan and Michael J. Rosen.

Reprinted with the permission of Simon & Schuster from *No Bad Dogs* by Barbara Woodhouse. Copyright © 1987 by Barbara Woodhouse.

Excerpt from *Lad: A Dog* by Albert Payson Terhune. Copyright © 1919, 1959 by E.P. Dutton, renewed 1987 by E.P. Dutton. Used by permission of Dutton Signet, a division of Penguin Books USA Inc.

Excerpt from *James Herriot's Dog Stories* by James Herriot. Copyright © 1986 by James Herriot. Reprinted with permission by St. Martin's Press Incorporated and Harold Ober Associates Inc.

Reprinted from *How to Live with a Neurotic Dog* by Stephen Baker, © 1988. Used with permission of Contemporary Books, Inc., Chicago.

Excerpt from "The Pet Department" by James Thurber. Copyright © 1931, 1959 James Thurber. From *The Owl in the Attic*, published by HarperCollins.

Excerpt from *The Fireside Book of Dog Stories*. Copyright © 1943 James Thurber. Copyright © 1971 Rosemary A. Thurber.

Excerpt from *Man Meets Dog* by Konrad Lorenz, translated by Marjorie Kerp. Copyright © 1953 by Konrad Lorenz. Reprinted by permission of Deutscher Taschenbuch Verlag GmbH & Co. KG and Kodansha Publishers.

art   credits